Rev. date: 08/24/2016

To order additional copies of this book, contact:
Xlibris
1-888-795-4274
www.Xlibris.com
Orders@Xlibris.com

How long have you been in the Navy? All me bloomin' life! Me mother was a mermaid, me father was King Neptune. I was born on the crest of a wave and rocked in the cradle of the deep. Seaweed and barnacles are me clothes. Every tooth in me head is a marlin-spike; the hair on me head is hemp. Every bone in me body is a spar, and when I spits, I spits tar! I'se hard, I is, I am, I are!

This Nautical Journey Belongs To

_____

The author of the poem "How Long Have You Been in the Navy?" is unknown. The poem honored in time and steeped in tradition can be found in *Reef Points*, the Midshipmen Handbook of the United States Naval Academy, which is published annually by and with permission of the Naval Institute Press. Young men and women are called to entrust this "table salt" to memory before venturing off to sea.

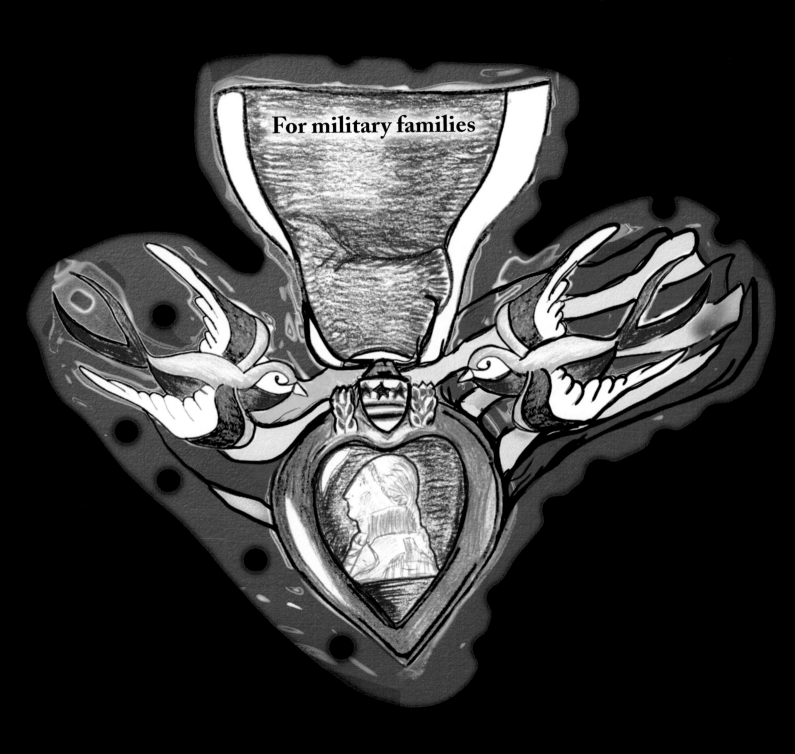

For military families

Illustrator's Note:

When I think of the question "How long have you been in the Navy?" it conjures up memories of chief initiation, midshipmen memorizing *Reef Points* in Bancroft Hall and the generations of individuals before me who have uttered those words. Most importantly, I think of my kids' smiling faces when they ask. "Dad, how long have you been in the Navy?" and I respond in my best pirate voice, "All me bloomin' life! Me mother was a mermaid, me father was King Neptune." They love the magic of those words. It was a way of sharing my military background with them in a tangible, educational way.

Born on the Crest of a Wave is a code shared by those who have chosen to defend our freedom. It is an escape from learning the mundane facts and the conventional requirements that all chiefs and officers should know. (Who is the Master Chief Petty Officer of the Navy? What are the standard commands for conning by compass heading? What are the material conditions of readiness? . . . and so on.)

Before sharing a piece of military history, please share what *Born on the Crest of a Wave* means to you.

How long have you been in the Navy?

_____

_____

_____

_____

_____

_____

_____

How long have you been in the Navy?

All me bloomin' life!

Me mother was a mermaid.

Note: **Mermaid** – (mur-meyd): (in folklore) a female marine creature, having the head, torso, and arms of a woman and the tail of a fish.

Me father was King Neptune.

NOTE: **Neptune** – (nep-toon): the ancient Roman god of the sea, identified with the Greek god Poseidon.

I was born on the crest of a wave . . .

NOTE: **Wave** – (weyv): a disturbance on the surface of a liquid body, as the sea or lake, in the form of a moving ridge or swell.

. . . and rocked in the cradle of the deep.

NOTE: **Cradle** – (kreyd-l): a small bed for an infant, usually on rockers.

Seaweed and barnacles are me clothes.

NOTE: **Seaweed** – (see-weed): any plant or plants growing in the ocean.

Barnacle – (bahr-nuh-kuh l): any marine crustaceans of the subclass *Cirripedia*, usually having a calcareous shell, being either stalked (goose barnacle) and attaching itself to ship bottoms and floating timber, or stalkless (rock barnacle or acorn barnacle) and attaching itself to rocks, especially in the intertidal zone.

Every tooth in me head is a marlin-spike.

NOTE: **Marlin-spike** – (mahr-lin-spahyk): a pointed iron implement used in separating the strands of rope in splicing, marling, etc.

13

The hair on me head is hemp.

NOTE: **Hemp** – (hemp): the tough fiber of this plant (*Cannabis Sativa*), used for making rope, coarse fabric, etc.

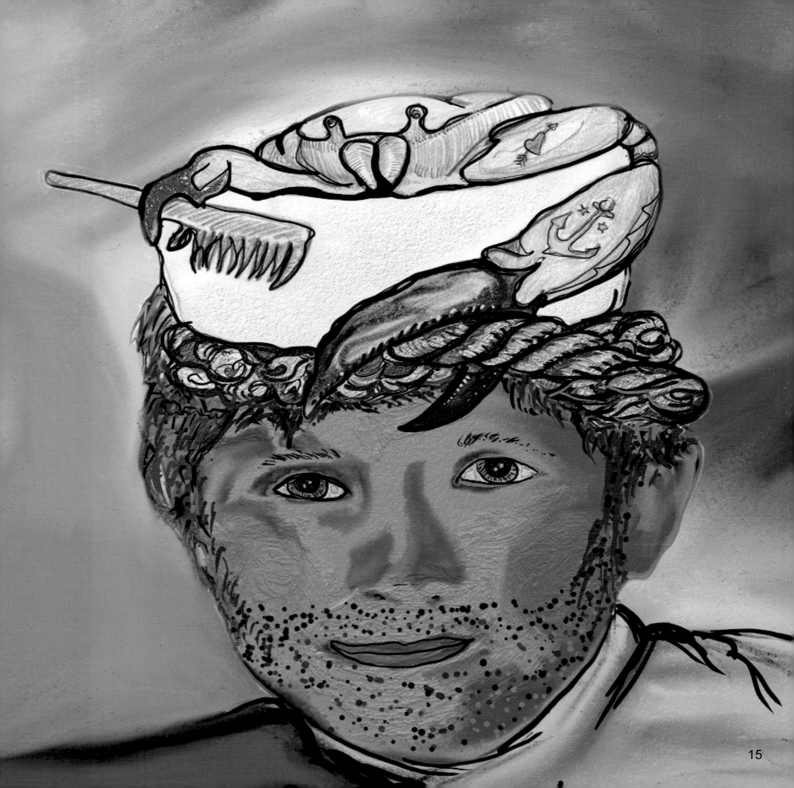

15

Every bone in me body is a spar . . .

NOTE: **Spar** – (spahr): a stout pole such as those used for masts, etc.; a mast, a yard, boom, gaff, or the like.

. . . and when I spits, I spits tar!

NOTE: **Tar** – (tahr): any of various dark-colored viscid products obtained by destructive distillation of certain organic substances, as coal or wood. Before the invention of waterproof fabrics, sailors used tar to waterproof their clothing.

I am,

I are!

• About the Illustrator •

Jonathan Kehoe is a 2001 graduate of the US Naval Academy (AUGHT-ONE). While at the Academy, he organized the first "Youngster Luau," which has become the custom celebratory event for third-class midshipmen during Commissioning Week. Following his days as a midshipman, Jonathan served in the US Navy aboard the *USS Guardian* as a Surface Warfare Officer and abroad as an Explosive Ordnance Disposal (EOD) Officer. In an effort to raise money and awareness for the EOD Memorial, Jonathan with the support of his team set the world record for the fastest mile in a bomb suit while serving in Iraq.

2009 World Record set in Iraq.

Navy EOD at work.
Hooyah EODMU 6.

Thank you for supporting the
EOD Warrior Foundation

A portion of the proceeds from this book will go to the EOD Warrior Foundation. Donations to this cause can be made through the Combined Federal Campaign (CFC) number 37190, at the website: www.eodwarriorfoundation.org, or by mail to: EOD Warrior Foundation 701 East John Sims Parkway, Suite 305, Niceville, FL 32578.

When you go home, tell them of us and say: For their tomorrow, we gave our today.

One of twelve epitaphs written by John Maxwell Edmonds (1875–1958) for those lost in World War I. The words are carved into a memorial honoring soldiers of the Second British Division, who fought during World War II. This memorial, which made these words famous, rests in Kohima, India.

Printed in the United States
by Baker & Taylor Publisher Services

The book, *Born on a Crest of a Wave*, illustrates a poem that men and women of the United States Navy have committed to memory for generations. Ask any sailor *How Long have you been in the Navy?* and a grin is sure to appear as he or she begins, "All me bloomin' life…" The book presents beautiful illustrations of the poem - King Neptune being pulled by seahorses, an octopus rocking a baby in the cradle of the deep, and a crab's barber shop deep below the ocean's surface.

Xlibris

ISBN 978-1-4990-2543-9

51599

9 781499 025439

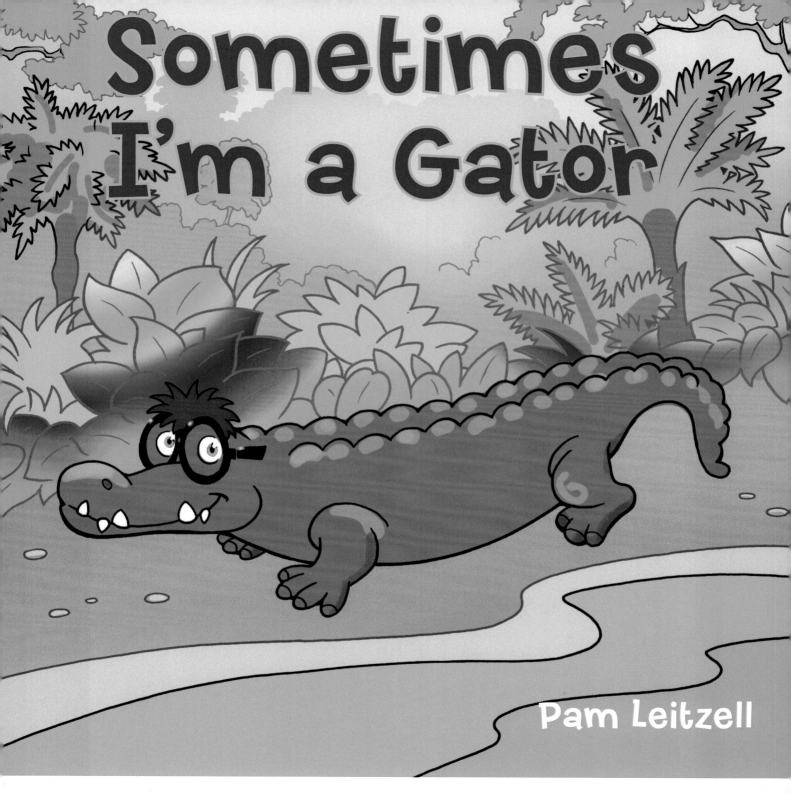

Sometimes I'm a Gator

Pam Leitzell